A Family for Tilly

Helping a Child with Reactive Attachment Disorder

Priscilla E. Jones

Copyright © 2014 Priscilla E Jones

All Rights Reserved. No part of this book may be reproduced or utilized in any form or by any means, electronic or mechanical, including photocopying, recording, or by any information storage and retrieval system, without permission in writing from the author.

PEJones.Publishing@gmail.com

ISBN-13: 978-1500612443

ISBN-10: 1500612448

DEDICATION

This book is dedicated to my wonderful Mother who taught me by example how to be a good person and a good parent.

This is a work of fiction. Names, characters, businesses, places, events and incidents are either the products of the author's imagination or used in a fictitious manner. Any resemblance to actual persons, living or dead, or actual events is purely coincidental.

CONTENTS

1. A New Daughter ?	1
2. Tilly	5
3. A Family of Four	11
4. A Family in Chaos	18
5. Christmas	26
6. Some Progress!	31
7. Reactive Attachment Disorder	39
8. Logical Consequences	44
9. Attachment	50
10. The Children's Hospital	56
11. Saying Good Bye	67
Epilogue	73
References	75

Chapter 1 - A New Daughter?

Tilly was a pretty little girl with brown wavy hair and dark brown eyes, but she had a rather frozen-looking, grim smile on her face. Hmmm.... I looked again at the photo our case worker had given us. Tilly was a four year-old girl who had just become available for adoption. I wondered if this little girl would be our new daughter. Would this child enjoy being part of our family? It was so hard to really know.....

We, my husband Bill, 9 year-old son Charlie, and I, had embarked on this adoptive journey over a year ago. We were hoping to find a little girl who needed a home and give Charlie a little sister. We had been told at the beginning of the process that we would have to take hours of pre-adoptive foster care classes, have a home evaluation and interviews, and then wait for a suitable child to become available.

After going through the long weekends of classes and meeting all of the state's requirements, we were finally ready to begin looking for our child. However, during the year of our search there had been only a few possible girls for us in the whole state, and each of these children had hundreds of prospective families interested in them.

Surprisingly, we had been one of the final three families for three of these girls, but each time another family had been chosen as the adoptive family. The agency thought the first child we had chosen wouldn't culturally fit into our mostly white, rural community, another little girl was determined to fit better into a family with no other children her age, and the girl that seemed like the best match for us was removed from availability at the last minute by the current foster parents, who decided to adopt her themselves.

I felt emotionally drained by this whole process. Whenever we found a child that we thought would work for us and were chosen as one of the final families, we would have to commit to the child based on a photo and a little background information. It was such a struggle to make this kind of final decision without knowing very much about the personality or life history of the child. Was this a little girl who would like to live on a farm, have a big brother, and be part of a busy family? Three times we had gone through the process and declared that we would commit to the child, only to be told later, sorry.

I wasn't sure that I wanted to try again. I studied the picture of Tilly and re-read the brief information that her case worker had provided. Tilly was currently living with relatives, enjoyed preschool, didn't have any major issues, and liked cats. That all sounded good, but why was I so bothered by her stiff smile in the photo? There was just something that didn't seem right........

The little girl was wearing turquoise shorts with a pink flowered top and was standing in front of a large hydrangea bush that was in full bloom. Maybe Tilly had been holding the smile for a long time before the photographer finally took the picture. Maybe she was a little shy and had been told sternly to "SMILE". It seemed so strange to me that adoptive families were forced to make a decision about a child before knowing if they would be the family chosen for the child, and without being able to actually meet the child that might soon become a part of their lives.

My husband thought the child would be fine, and my son thought so too. We were all rather exhausted from our long search and these difficult decisions, but finally decided that our answer would be yes. We told the case worker we would like to be considered as the home for Tilly, but we also decided that this would be our last try. I updated our family photo album that would be used at the adoption placement meeting to help the panel decide which family would be the best for Tilly, gave it to our case worker, and then tried to not think about the outcome.

Our family had a trip to the Midwest coming up and this made an excellent diversion for us. We had a wonderful time on our trip visiting our relatives and had decided not to worry about things back home. We had given the adoption process our best shot and would just wait to see what would happen.

A few days after we returned from our trip, we received a call from our case worker. This time we were the family that was chosen!! Tilly would be our new little girl!!!!! We couldn't believe it! Wow!!!

We asked about the process to meet Tilly and start the transition of her move to our home. Our case worker explained that the child's case worker would be in charge of the transition and we should contact him to get things started. I called right away and was told by Tilly's case worker that he would be out of town for a few weeks, but that we could go meet Tilly whenever we were ready and then work out a transition schedule with the aunt and uncle she was living with. We were surprised by his lack of involvement, but we called Tilly's relatives and made plans to visit her that weekend.

As we made the several hours trip to see Tilly for the first time, I was feeling very apprehensive. The child we were about to meet was going to be my new daughter. What if I didn't like her? What if she didn't like me? Had this really been such a good idea? Our family was doing fine already. Why were we plunging into this unknown situation?

Chapter 2 - Tilly

As Bill parked our car in front of the house, I tried to calm myself down. Charlie, who was in the back seat, suddenly became very quiet. I wondered what he was thinking. He had been an only child for 9 years. He must be wondering what it would be like to have a little sister.....

Suddenly the front door of the house burst open and a little girl with long, tussled light brown hair ran outside. There she was! Tilly and an older, blonde-haired girl were playing with a doll stroller. As we got out of the car, I could see that there was a cat sitting in the stroller that didn't seem to mind taking a ride. We said "Hi" to the girls and then rang the door bell. Tilly's aunt and uncle invited us inside and we sat down and introduced ourselves.

It has been six years since that first day we met Tilly, but somehow every detail is so clear. I remember so well how I felt sitting in that living room, looking over at the couple who had cared for our new little girl for the past two years. A silence had fallen after our introductions. I think that we all felt slightly uncomfortable that there was no professional there to help lead us through this process. We asked a few questions about how Tilly had come to live with them and then, eager to spend time with our new daughter, asked if we could take Tilly to McDonald's for some ice cream so we could all get acquainted.

Tilly's aunt and uncle thought that sounded fine and the aunt went outside to call her in. Tilly soon popped into the living room still pushing the doll buggy, which was by this time without its passenger. Charlie, Bill, and I introduced ourselves and told her that we were going to be her new family. Tilly said she already knew that and ran into the next room and returned with our adoption photo album. She said she had been looking at our pictures and had known who we were as soon as we got out of our car. Tilly liked the idea of going to go get some ice cream, so we piled into our car and set off.

When we got to McDonald's, we all ordered ice cream and then wandered into the play area of the restaurant. Charlie and Tilly soon finished their treats and began climbing the play structure and sliding down the slide one after the other. As I watched the two of them playing together, I tried to wrap my mind around the fact that we now had two children.

It's one thing to plan for a new child, but quite another to have her right there in front of you laughing and playing. It was so exciting and scary at the same time. I felt wonder and joy, but somehow it was very hard to grasp this new situation so suddenly. After a while Tilly came over to me and leaned against my legs. It seemed so natural to just lift her up onto my lap. She looked up at me and gave me a hesitant smile. Then she leaned up against me and seemed to just melt. I wrapped my arms around her and something in my heart just melted too.

This was our girl, my child! I felt a surge of protectiveness as I held her close. In that moment our lives seemed to join together and I felt an amazingly powerful bond to my new daughter. Tilly looked up again and gave me a big, rather relieved-looking grin. Her dark eyes, which had looked rather suspiciously at us before, now appeared accepting. She seemed like she was relaxing for the first time in a long time and was so happy to just be with me and feel so safe. I don't remember exactly how long she sat with me, but the close feelings we shared at that moment affected both of us very deeply. In the months to come, that bond would be tested but would always survive.

Since our first meeting had gone so well, we decided it would be a good idea to bring Tilly to our house for a few hours later in the week so she could see her new home. It seemed like it would an easier transition for Tilly if she was able to see her new house and then move in a few days later. Tilly's aunt and uncle agreed to our plan so we arranged to pick her up on Saturday, in the morning, and have our new daughter spend the day with us.

Now that I had met Tilly, I had a better idea about what she was like and decided to buy her some new clothes and a few toys. It was so much fun to pick out some pretty dresses and shorts outfits for her and choose some cute stuffed animals, one with a pink bow around its neck. Shopping for a little girl was so much more fun than buying the same old jeans and shirts that Charlie always wore. There was so much variety in the girls department!

Tilly was waiting for us when we drove down to pick her up that Saturday and happily came with us to see her new home. On the drive home we talked about our animals and answered her questions about her new room and new house. Tilly saw some cows out of the car window and said she remembered helping her dad feed the cows on the farm they lived on when she was very little. We were surprised that she could remember something so well that had happened when she wasn't even two years old. She certainly had quite a memory!

When we arrived at our house, Tilly jumped out and ran around the huge back yard. She then saw Charlie's big wooden play structure and Charlie helped her climb up into the tower. We all sat outside for awhile eating strawberry popsicles and then invited Tilly inside to see the house. Tilly liked her new room and immediately wanted to put on the new outfit lying on her bed. She changed into the little lilac overall shorts with the matching shirt and gave me a huge grin. "I"m going to like it here," she announced.

We showed her all around our rather strange, tall house, with its two long staircases. We also introduced her to our collie, Kelly, and the horses up at the barn. Tilly took everything in and seemed genuinely happy. Before we drove her back to her aunt and uncle's house, we went for a quick walk in the woods that surrounds the back yard.

Bill took our picture as Charlie stood holding his homemade wooden axe that he had been showing Tilly and I held my new daughter in my arms. When I look at that picture now, I see the hopeful smiles on all three of our faces. We were all starting down a new path and trying to adjust to this new family that was forming.

Since the transition seemed to be going well for Tilly, we all agreed that our new daughter would move in with us the following week. I called her aunt and uncle the morning we would be picking her up to make sure that they thought she was ready for this final step. Tilly's aunt said that Tilly had been sitting on the curb in front of the house since early that morning and was just waiting for us to come to get her.

I was surprised that this 4 year-old girl was so eager to leave the home where she had lived for over two years. From our foster care parenting classes, we had learned that children were usually very reluctant to leave their care givers, especially if they had lived there for any length of time. What was making this tiny girl so anxious to come to our house?

When we arrived to pick up Tilly, there she was standing in the middle of the front yard. "I've been waiting here for a long time," she told us. We asked if she was all packed up and she showed us some garbage bags that were tied up in front of the house. Her aunt and uncle then came out to meet us and explained that Tilly had more things in her room. I followed the aunt into the house and down the stairs where there were more big, black, partially-filled garbage bags sitting in the middle of a small bedroom.

    While I stood looking around at Tilly's room, the aunt took everything remaining in Tilly's closet and tossed it into an open bag. Child-sized clothes hangers, a sock, parts of toys, and some clothes disappeared into the sack. I remember thinking how strange it was that nothing was being sorted or folded. Tilly's belongings were being treated just like, well, garbage. I didn't say anything but just helped haul the bags upstairs so that Bill and Charlie could then load them into the back of our pickup truck.

    Everyone else stayed upstairs talking while Tilly and I went back down to look around her room one last time. I wanted to make sure there wasn't anything that she had forgotten. As we walked around the room looking in the closet and under the bed, Tilly told me that her room had originally been built as a playroom for her cousin, Sarah, and that her cousin had been very upset when she came to live there and needed the room as a bedroom. Tilly looked around to make sure that we were alone, and then said, "Sarah told me that she's glad she's going to get her other room back now."

    My little girl took another look around the room, and then looked up at me and said, "I'm ready to go." In the weeks and months to come, I would learn more and more about the struggles Tilly had while living in this house. I would also come to understand why her aunt and uncle didn't seem very sad that she was leaving.......

Chapter 3 - A Family of Four

Tilly settled right into the family as fast as she settled into her new room. She loved her closet full of new, pretty clothes and shelves where she could set out her toys. As we unpacked her things from the garbage bags, I was amazed to find that she only had three socks. Somehow that really struck me. How could a child get by with only three socks? We went out right away and bought more socks and Tilly also picked out some new tennis shoes since the only shoes she had that still fit were some sandals. As I put her new socks and shoes away after our shopping trip, Tilly twirled around smiling in her new room.

One of the first days Tilly was with us, it was warm so we filled up the wading pool outside in the back yard under one of our large fir trees. It was a shady place to play and also a spot I could easily see from the kitchen window. As I washed the breakfast dishes, I could see Tilly and Charlie as they splashed happily in the pool and then ran over to the play structure to try to slide down the slide in their wet suits. Charlie showed Tilly how he could run up the slide too.

We ended up spending that whole warm July day just enjoying ourselves in the shady yard. Late that afternoon, Tilly announced, "I sure like having a brother!" Charlie grinned at both of us as from his "fort" at the top of the play structure where he was sitting with our collie. Charlie looked like he was enjoying having a new sister too.

We had been told that children who have been in foster care take awhile to adjust to their new families, so we were expecting Tilly to have some separation anxiety about leaving her previous home. Surprisingly, Tilly didn't seem to miss her aunt and uncle at all. She didn't even seem interested in talking to them on the phone.

We had been advised to keep up phone contact with the aunt and uncle for awhile, to help ease the transition for Tilly, but soon stopped trying to get her to speak to them. We continued to call them for a few days to let them know how she was doing, but they didn't seem interested in maintaining a connection either. This was puzzling to me, but since everything was going well, I didn't worry about it too much.

I did speak to a case worker about a week after Tilly arrived while we were attending a picnic arranged for foster children in our area. I asked if it was a problem that Tilly had so immediately accepted us as her family. The case worker simply said how lucky for us that things were going well. She didn't seem to be concerned at all.

For the first few weeks, it did seem like we had transformed fairly effortlessly into a family of four. Tilly accompanied us to several social events and our friends were astonished that this little girl seemed to fit so perfectly into our lives. I remember saying she was like "a daughter out of a box." Tilly arrived, adjusted quickly to her new environment, and was happy. With her dark brown eyes, and light brown, wavy hair, she even looked a lot like me. Charlie was happy to have a new little sister to show off for and teach important things like how to play soccer and climb a tree. Bill was very proud, too, of his expanded family and loved seeing the two children playing together.

This idyllic family situation lasted almost a month, but then things began to change. Tilly seemed very suddenly to start having trouble with our household rules. She loved her pretty, new room, but would no longer pick up her toys or crayons at the end of the day. When I was firm about helping out, she would become violent and would throw toys at the walls, at me or down the stairs. I thought she was probably getting overwhelmed by all the changes in her life and tried to be very patient with her. I would try to get her to just attempt to do what I was asking, such as to pick up just one toy, but my request was met with dark, unblinking eyes that would just stare at me as I spoke.

It was a strange, haunting look that I would see when Tilly was being uncooperative. There was no understanding, no reaction to me at these times when she was angry--just a dark, blank glare, in an expressionless face. I had never seen anyone look at me that way and I didn't know what to think. It seemed as if she was daring me to do something--throw toys back at her, yell at her, or explode into anger. When Tilly would give me that awful blank glare, it seemed like there was no way to reach her. Even though we were standing in the same room, it was as though she was a huge distance away. I had no idea what to do or how I could help my little girl, but I knew that something very strange was going on.

About this same time, Tilly also began exhibiting another very odd behavior. When not allowed to do what she wanted, or when sent to her room for a short time-out she would pick up a book, rock back and forth on her knees and chant in a monotone about how mean we were to her and how unhappy she was. She would keep up the chanting while turning the pages of the book and would keep going for long periods of time, even after I would go up and tell her that she could come out of her room again. She didn't seem upset while she was talking to herself in this flat, strange voice, but would just rock back and forth, for sometimes an hour or more, and seemed to be a world away.

Another development, that was very worrying to me, began a few months after Tilly came to live with us. Tilly was becoming increasingly aggressive towards Charlie and our pets. Tilly had not been physically aggressive to her cousin or the cat in her previous home, so I couldn't understand why it was happening here. Charlie continued to be very helpful and nice to his new little sister, but Tilly seemed to become more and more angry at Charlie. On several occasions she had tried to push him down the stairs and recently had tried to hit him over the head with her rake while we were all up in the garden. Another time, when the kids had gone shopping with Bill, Tilly smashed a shopping cart into Charlie and that time Charlie had gotten hurt.

Charlie was older and able to fend off most of these attacks, but he was becoming very depressed that things at home were now so chaotic. Charlie told me that sometimes when we were all in the living room, he would look up from his book to see Tilly looking at him with "angry, dark eyes". "It's like she wants me to die," he told me, sadly. "Why does she keep doing that?" I had no answer for him, but I promised him that we would fix things, somehow.

Of course, as a mother, I wanted to protect Charlie from this angry little person, but other than always being watchful when they were together, I wasn't sure how to do that. I attempted to get Tilly to stop her mean glares at Charlie by making her leave the room whenever I caught her doing it, but still Tilly persisted. I made sure that I didn't leave the kids in the house by themselves and would wait until Bill came home from work before going outside or up to the barn. It was so hard to keep a constant vigilance, yet I knew I needed to be very watchful to keep Charlie safe.

One time I left the family room for a minute, and when I came back, Tilly was coming up behind Charlie with a pair of scissors held like a dagger. We tried to keep everything out of her reach that could be dangerous, but occasionally she would find something to use as a weapon. How could we allow Tilly to stay if we couldn't get these attacks to stop? I knew that Tilly was in desperate need of help herself, but had no idea what to do. How could such a young person have so much anger inside?

I had contacted our case worker as soon as these problems started and told her that we needed some help. I explained that Tilly was becoming very aggressive towards Charlie as well as becoming more and more defiant. The case worker listened, but said she couldn't really offer any help. I was shocked at her response and reminded her that we had been told in our pre-adoptive training classes that most children in the state system would need counseling, which the state would provide. I insisted that she immediately make an appointment for us with a counselor.

Our case worker scheduled a meeting for us with a social worker who worked for the county that next week. The social worker talked to Tilly and me for about half an hour and agreed that Tilly was having some big problems. She also said, after Tilly had left the room, that the adoption probably wouldn't be successful without counseling. She then proceeded to tell me that our county didn't have counseling available for foster children any more unless the child was suicidal or psychotic. She explained that in the past they had always offered family counseling to families adopting children from the state but, unfortunately, no longer had the funding to do so.

The social worker finished by saying that she was sorry, but the county wouldn't be able to help us. She then suggested that I find a private counselor for Tilly who would accept the insurance the state provided for foster children. When I explained to her how unhappy Charlie was with this new little sister who seemed to hate him and who kept attacking him, she suggested that I take Charlie to a counselor too. As I left the building with Tilly, I felt like we had been completely abandoned. Why wouldn't this agency who had given us our little girl help us? How would it help anyone if this adoption didn't work out?

Over the next few weeks I tried unsuccessfully to find a psychologist or counselor that accepted Tilly's insurance plan. The few that did take this insurance said they had reached their quota of state clients and couldn't take on any more. After my futile attempt to find professional help for Tilly, I called our caseworker to express my frustration. How were we supposed to manage? How would we ever be able to adopt Tilly when we had no idea how to help her? Our case worker said the state would pay for a mental health and physical evaluation at the University Children's Hospital for Tilly, but the wait for an appointment was usually at least 6 months. I asked her to go ahead and put us on the list, but I felt like any help we had to wait 6 months for would be too little, too late.

I was finally able to find a child psychologist who agreed to see Charlie. Our son was covered by our family's private insurance so there were more providers available. I was thinking that this psychologist would not only be able to help Charlie feel better, but would also be able to give us some advice about Tilly. Charlie's appointment was a few weeks away and I hoped that we would now be able to get some help for our family.

Chapter 4 - A Family in Chaos

It was well into Fall now, and Charlie was back in school. He was in the third grade this year, and had a wonderful teacher who really seemed to like him. I was hoping that a good atmosphere at school would help offset the miserable time he was having at home. We also found a preschool for Tilly to attend 3 days a week, and I was hoping that more structured days for the kids would help all of us.

Finally, the day arrived to meet with Charlie's psychologist. I explained the situation that we were having with Tilly and how sad and frustrated Charlie had become. The psychologist was an older woman, who seemed a bit distant, but she listened and seemed to understand our situation. I was very hopeful that she would be able to help us.

Charlie began having weekly therapy sessions, but unfortunately the sessions didn't seem to be helping and he and I were becoming very discouraged. Charlie reported that the psychologist wouldn't talk to him much during their hour together, but instead just asked him to select carved wooden animals and objects from her huge collection and place them in a large sand tray. At the end of the session she would ask him a few questions about his placement of the objects and then tell him he could leave.

Charlie said she didn't give him any advice or suggestions about how to get along with his sister, and he didn't understand how putting animals in the sand was supposed to help.

After one of his sessions, I asked the psychologist if she could work with Tilly and Charlie together occasionally to help their relationship. She gave me a rather funny look and said that wouldn't be possible due to Tilly's lack of insurance. I then asked the psychologist if she could offer any suggestions to me on how to help Tilly. This woman had years of experience with children, so she should certainly be able to give me some good ideas on how to manage our difficult child. The psychologist merely told me to read a book on child development. I couldn't believe her answer!

I had really been counting on the psychologist's help to find some way to change Tilly's behavior. I wondered if this professional had any concern at all for the young clients she was supposed to be helping. I knew nothing about counseling but thought working with the whole family or helping the siblings learn to get along would be a part of any type of therapy for a formerly happy child who was now under attack by a new member of the family.

Tilly's behavior by this time was becoming harder and harder for me to deal with. I had to watch her all the time now, even when Charlie wasn't home, because she had gotten so she would break or destroy whatever she could reach. I had started removing things from her room early on when she began refusing to pick things up, figuring it would be easier for her with just a few toys to take care of. This plan hadn't worked. Tilly continued to smash and break even the few toys that she had left. Over time, we ended up taking out almost everything from her room except for her bed, clothes and her book shelf. I made sure she had a book to look at and a coloring book, but that was it. Finally one day I had to remove her book shelf, too, because she refused to stop scribbling all over it with her crayons.

Tilly also was having trouble at mealtimes. In our house, we usually ate dinner each night all together, at the dining table. One of the first things we noticed about Tilly at meal times was that she had absolutely no table manners. She wouldn't hold her fork like most people do, instead she would use the fork as a shovel and push food off her plate directly into her mouth. Sometimes she would just use her hands to feed herself. As we taught her how to correctly use silverware (and a napkin!) I asked if her aunt and uncle had tried to show her the same thing. Tilly surprised us with her answer.

Apparently while living with her relatives, she would usually eat a microwaved frozen dinner (or in Tilly's terms, a dinner from a box) downstairs in front of a TV while the rest of the family ate upstairs at the table. Tilly said simply, "That's the way it always was." This certainly explained Tilly's eating style! I tried not to question Tilly about her life with her aunt and uncle, but as she mentioned things on her own, it became apparent that Tilly was never a part of that family. She was taken care of, but never, it seemed, actually cared for.

The other issue we had at mealtimes was Tilly's attempt to control everyone. She would often ask to have a dish of food passed to her, and then when it was there in front of her, she would say she didn't want any. She also seemed to be constantly spilling her milk, creating a commotion that she really seemed to enjoy. Sometimes Tilly would just sit at the table, refuse to eat anything and then ask for something different for supper, something that wasn't being served that night. At first I would try to accommodate her demands, but eventually I learned that even when I brought her what she was asking for, she would refuse to eat that, too. Tilly seemed to enjoy having people get things for her that she could then decide she didn't want. She also seemed amused whenever she "accidentally" spilled her glass of milk and disrupted everyone else's meal.

I didn't want mealtimes to be so chaotic, so I finally made some new rules. Tilly's glass of milk would now stay on the counter and she could go over and get a drink when she needed one. I also said that if Tilly didn't like what we were having for dinner or began causing trouble, she would need to leave the table and then come back after the rest of us had finished and have some cereal and carrots by herself. Tilly seemed disappointed that her dinnertime fun was over, but the rest of us appreciated the new rules. Sometimes our daughter would eat dinner nicely with us, and at other times, she would be sent from the table and would eat later by herself.

As soon as I had learned that Tilly would be coming to live with us, I had been trying to figure out how I could take care of my horses every morning and still keep an eye on a preschooler. When Charlie had been young, his grandmother had watched him in the mornings, long enough for me to do all my barn chores. That wasn't an option now, so I had to come up with some other plan. I finally decided that the best option would be to fix up an empty stall in the barn as a play room for Tilly. I cleaned the stall well, found a comfy chair she could sit in with a blanket for when it was chilly, brought in some toys and moved our pet rabbit, Velvet, and his cage there too.

    At first Tilly had enjoyed coming with me up to the barn. She'd help me clean stalls for awhile and would sometimes want to sit on one of the horses. Eventually, she would decide to go to her "play room" and play with the rabbit.

    Later, though, as time went on, Tilly became unhappy when I needed to go to the barn. She'd complain about having to go outside when it was cold and would try to hurt the rabbit when she didn't think I was looking. I quickly relocated Velvet to a safer place and later had to remove all the toys from the play room as well. Tilly, at times, would go into a rage and scream about how much she hated the barn. She would hurl anything within reach against the walls, which resulted in smashed toys and dirty, crumpled dolls. Reasoning and talking to Tilly didn't seem to do any good. I finally learned to just put Tilly in her chair, wrap the blanket around her if it was cold, and tell her she had to stay there until I was finished. I could usually get done in about 10 minutes and was rather surprised that she would actually stay in her chair until I was finished. My little four year-old might shout the whole time we were at the barn, but she did stay put.

As Charlie and I became more and more frustrated with Tilly's extreme behavior, I began talking more seriously to Bill about my concerns with adopting Tilly. I had already asked the case worker to stop the adoption proceedings, for awhile, so that we could try to resolve some of Tilly's issues. Late in the evening, after the kids had gone to bed, I would try to explain to Bill that I didn't think this child was going to work out for our family.

Bill did seem sorry that Charlie was being constantly attacked and was so unhappy, but he said that Tilly was his daughter and she was going to stay. I tried to help Bill see the difficulties in going forward with the adoption of a child who was getting more and more out of control, but he refused to consider any option other than keeping her. I could not understand Bill's determination to adopt Tilly when it seemed to be destroying our family, but I decided that I'd just have to try to help her quickly so that Charlie wouldn't unravel in the process.

I have a background in science and animal behavior and when I couldn't understand Tilly's behavior, I took a scientific approach and began to methodically write down what happened each day. I was hoping that writing things down would somehow give me some understanding about what was going on, so that I could figure out how to help Tilly and our family. To make things clearer for Tilly, I tried very hard to be extremely firm with rules and equally rewarding whenever Tilly made even a tiny effort to be cooperative. I wanted to make doing the right thing very obvious, and as easy as possible for my little girl. It was depressing for me, though, to have to be so rigid. I felt, at times, like a jail warden, always having to be on alert and watchful of this little person in our home.

As the months went by and I was looking back through my journal, one pattern I noticed was that on the days that Tilly wore one of her pretty dresses to preschool, her behavior would be especially bad. On these days she would be extremely uncooperative in every way. She would sometimes throw her sack lunch at me on the drive to preschool, kick very hard as I tried to help her put on her shoes, shout all the way to school and argue with everything that I said.

I thought and thought, but couldn't figure out how wearing pretty clothes could result in such angry behavior. Tilly really liked picking out an outfit for school each day, and just loved the dresses with ruffles and decorations. Finally, though, I remembered that Tilly had once mentioned that her aunt would pay more attention to her when they all got dressed up to go somewhere together. Her aunt would help her fix her hair and find nice clothes for her to wear when they were going to some special family or social event.

Somehow, wearing the pretty dresses I had bought her for school seemed to trigger some angry emotions, possibly bringing back some unhappy memories. As soon as I figured this out, I put away the dresses, except for one she could wear when she wanted to play dress up, and bought her some nice jeans and tops for school. Although there was a lot of complaining and whining about not having the dresses to wear, this change made a huge difference in her behavior on school days.

    While I was very glad to have found a way to make getting ready for school easier for both of us, I knew that I was in way over my head with this child! Taking care of Tilly and trying to protect Charlie and our pets was exhausting, emotionally draining, and heart-breaking, but because of Bill's insistence that Tilly stay, I didn't feel like I had any other choice than to just keep trying. I redoubled my efforts to try to make my expectations very clear for Tilly and hoped that somehow, someday things would get better.

Chapter 5 - Christmas

As Christmas approached, we began decorating the house for the holidays. I wasn't sure how the holiday season would affect Tilly, but I hoped she would enjoy our family traditions. Every year we would hang long garlands along the upstairs balcony swagged up every few feet with big bows. I just loved looking up at those garlands from downstairs; it made the whole house feel festive. We also had decorations that we would hang above the piano and over the doorway. Each year, about the middle of December, we would put our huge Christmas tree in the corner of the living room and cover it with ornaments and the decorations that Charlie had made at school. As much fun as it was to decorate the house, one of my favorite parts of the holiday season was baking lots of cookies and banana bread to send to all our relatives and to give to our neighbors.

Tilly actually did pretty well with all the holiday commotion and enjoyed all the decorations. She was fascinated by the Christmas tree and kept wanting to pull down ornaments and pull on the branches. I ended up marking off an area around the tree with masking tape and told her not to cross the tape line on the carpet. Surprisingly, Tilly was able to follow this rule very well, so I was able to do some baking in the kitchen and keep an eye on her in the living room without worrying that she might get hurt by pulling the tree down on top of herself.

One morning a few days before Christmas I ran outside for something and came back in to see Tilly whacking our glass-topped coffee table with a toy metal hammer. She was banging hard with lots of energy as if she wanted to break the thick glass. I stopped her and asked why she was trying to break the table. Tilly turned slowly around and looked at me. Then she answered, "It's not you guys. You all are nice to me..... I'm just mad...... inside...... all by myself." I was stunned by this response. I didn't know what to say. Our troubled little girl was trying to describe to me the anger she had been feeling inside for so long.. What an insightful answer from this little 4 ½ year old.

My mind was racing as I tried to think of some way to help Tilly deal with this strong emotion she had just shared with me. After thinking for a minute, I took her hand and suggested that we go up to her room. When we were upstairs I took out a piece of notebook paper and her crayons. "Do you want to draw a picture of your parents?' I asked. It seemed like she needed to express something from her past, and I guessed that it might be about her mom and dad. They had left her when she was only two years old, and there must be some very strong feelings there. Maybe the holidays had brought up some memories that were painful to her.

Tilly sat down with the paper and drew a man and a woman. When she was finished she showed me that she had drawn the man with big, round blue eyes. Tilly explained, "Sometimes when Daddy came home, his eyes would be all blue. There wouldn't be any white." I knew both of her parents had been drug users which might explain why her dad's eyes had looked so strange. I was amazed that she would have noticed this small detail and remembered it such a long time later.

    I asked Tilly if she wanted to say anything to the people in her picture. I wasn't sure if this was really the right thing to do, but it seemed like she needed to get something out that she was feeling. She hadn't seen her parents in such a long time and there must be so many things that she'd never been able to tell them. Tilly didn't answer my question or say anything at all. She just kept looking at her drawing.

    I can recall those moments with Tilly in her room so vividly.....the little girl sitting completely still, just staring at her drawing. She was in so much pain and I felt so powerless to help her. I sat with her awhile and then went downstairs so she could be alone. Later I found little pieces of torn up notebook paper behind her bed. I didn't mention the picture again, and neither did Tilly.

    As Christmas drew nearer, Bill and I each took the kids Christmas shopping to buy things for the family. We gave each child some money and then helped them figure out how much things cost. Charlie was quite competent with money and was a careful shopper. He had learned long ago how to compare prices and make the most of his birthday and Christmas money. Tilly had never had her own money to spend before, except maybe a few coins to buy some candy. At first, as I was helping her shop, she kept wanting to buy things for herself, but finally she figured out what to buy for Charlie and Bill. Bill took her shopping another time to buy something for me.

Christmas, that year with Tilly, was an extravagant event. We had bought her and Charlie plenty of presents but hadn't expected the many more that came for both of them from her biological grandparents, as well as from my family. It seemed to take hours to open everything. Tilly was amazed that she had so many new toys, and right away I could see that this was probably too much of a good thing. We had Tilly pick a few favorites, which included a huge wooden barn with stalls and horses, and some new crayons and coloring books. We told her we would put the rest of her gifts away for awhile and Tilly was actually OK with this. She was a very smart little girl and seemed to understand that things were easier for her when there weren't too many toys to take care of.

I think Tilly really enjoyed watching all of us open the presents she had picked out for us as we sat around the tree that morning. Her eyes were shining and she had a huge smile on her face as she bounced up and down urging us to tear off the paper and see what was inside the gifts. She had gotten me a small, light brown stuffed dog with floppy ears that was wearing a santa hat and red neck scarf. Tilly was just inches away from me as I unwrapped the cute, fuzzy dog and wanted to know immediately if I liked it. "I love it," I said, as I gave her a hug. She then looked rather longingly at the stuffed dog that I was holding, as though maybe she wanted it herself. I told her it was a special present from her and I would always keep it and remember that she gave it to me on our first Christmas together. Hearing how important her present was seemed to make a difference to Tilly, and she went back to admiring her own gifts.

Chapter 6 - Some Progress!

As life went on for all of us, I did find some things to be encouraged about with our little girl. I had made it my mission to be very firm about things and to not give in to tantrums, screaming, or destruction. I knew, from my years of working with horses and dogs, that it was much easier to learn if the right choice was always right, and the wrong choice was always wrong. The child development books I had read recently also agreed with this theory. They stated that it was much easier for a child if the parents were firm with rules so that the child didn't have to constantly test the boundaries.

I knew we had made some good progress when one day, after I had told Tilly that she couldn't do something, she said, "Mommy when you say 'No', you never change your mind." I was thrilled that she was realizing this! I was so happy that I had managed to be so consistent! I felt like picking Tilly up and twirling her around, but instead, just agreed with her, that it was true I didn't change my mind. I had a smile on my face for a long time after hearing those words.

Another bright spot with Tilly was helping her learn to read. One evening she and I were home alone and I decided to get out one of Charlie's Dr. Seuss books. I asked Tilly if she wanted to hear a story and she quickly agreed. As I read the first few pages of *Hop on Pop* to her, I pointed to each word as I said it out loud. Then I started the book over and suggested that she read with me.

Tilly was a very smart girl, but she picked up reading much faster than I thought anyone could. After seeing the words just a few times, she could read without any help from me. Tilly had been in preschool for several years, so she did know the alphabet, but being able to remember and sound out the words so fast was amazing! Tilly was so excited and proud of herself! I was excited too. We were finally putting her quick and intelligent mind to work in a very positive way. We decided that we definitely should have some ice cream to celebrate.

Although the county couldn't provide any counseling for Tilly, I did get a call one day from the county social worker. She told me about a Federally funded study that was beginning for children Tilly's age who were defiant and asked if I was interested. "Yes!" I answered. She gave me a phone number, and I called right away to sign up.

I took Tilly for her evaluation later that week. I had been told that the evaluation, which involved asking me questions and observing the child, would last about an hour. Surprisingly, after only 10 minutes the evaluator said that Tilly would qualify for the study. Apparently, our little girl easily fit the oppositional/defiant diagnosis that they were looking for. We were told that half of the children would act as controls and the other half would be in the group whose parents would receive training on a new type of play therapy. I hoped we'd be in the training group, and luckily that's how it turned out.

As part of the training group, I was taught a method of playing with Tilly called Parent-Child Interactive Therapy. A trainer taught me to give positive comments, reflect aloud about what I saw Tilly doing during the play time, copy what Tilly was doing, and make descriptive comments about what Tilly was doing as she played. I was to do each of these things at least 10 times during our 5 minute "special play times" that we'd have every day. It took a little practice and coaching, but I learned the procedure and soon began having special play time with Tilly at home every afternoon.

Tilly loved our special play time together, and after a few weeks, I began to notice a change in the way she would talk to herself when she was playing on her own. My daughter had always talked while she was playing, but now instead of saying unhappy things and having the toys attack each other, I would hear her repeat things I had said to her during our play time. She would say, "I have lots of ideas" or "I know just where this should go" as she moved her toy animals happily around on the carpet. I was amazed that this "self talk" going on in her mind seemed to be changing. This play therapy stuff seemed to be making a difference!

All of the parents in the training group had been told that the second part of the Parent-Child training involved giving the child small commands during the special play time that would need to be followed. The idea was that as the child became good at following commands during special play time, it would transfer to the rest of the day. This sounded like something that might really help manage Tilly's behavior and I was anxious to try it. Unfortunately, since we were all part of a research study, Tilly and I could not begin this part of the training for 12 weeks. All of the participants had to do each part of the play therapy for the same amount of time so that the results could be analyzed later. I certainly understood keeping things consistent for the research project, but I needed something to help me with Tilly soon.

    Charlie had not gotten any help from his first psychologist, so we tried seeing a new one at a different clinic. This time Charlie had a male therapist, and I hoped this man would find a way to help Charlie deal with his increasing sadness about his life. Charlie had told me one evening before he went to bed, that he didn't want to have different parents, but he didn't really want to live at our house anymore.

    Charlie was also being bullied at school by a group of third grade boys and found no relief when he came home because of Tilly. Tilly wasn't attacking him anymore physically, but she just didn't seem to be able to tolerate having him anywhere near her. If he was reading in the living room and she came in to play with a toy, pretty soon Charlie would be complaining that he couldn't read because she was glaring at him.

    I had seen some of these interactions from the kitchen, and it happened just as Charlie described. Tilly would be playing with a toy or coloring but would frequently look up and stare with a hateful, fixed gaze right at Charlie. I had received this look before too, on many occasions, but usually because I had told Tilly she couldn't do what she was wanting to do. I wasn't sure why she would look this way at Charlie when he was just reading or playing with toys by himself. My son couldn't take all that angry energy focused right at him and he'd ask her to stop.

Tilly did seem like she was trying to cooperate. She actually would look away for awhile, but soon would be focusing on him again. I would also ask her to stop, and when she didn't, I would send her to her room for a time-out. If Tilly screamed and yelled in her room, I'd take her to the laundry room for her time-out instead, where her shouting didn't bother us as much. I talked to Tilly over and over about her behavior towards Charlie and how we all had to be nice to each other, but somehow, she didn't seem to be able or willing to change.

Charlie also started having severe growing pains in his legs, right when all these other problems were happening. His legs seemed to hurt the most in the mornings and sometimes, as I drove him to school and he was crying out in pain, Tilly would be laughing at him and mocking him from the back seat. He then went off to school to be taunted and picked on by the bullies. It was no wonder that he was so depressed! We had talked to his teacher and the principal about the bullies, but nothing seemed to be changing there.

In the evenings, after Tilly had gone to bed and Bill was letting the dog out, Charlie could finally have some time alone with me to talk about things that were bothering him. One night Charlie told me that he didn't really want to die, but if someone in the family needed to, he hoped it would be him. I hugged him close and told him how much I loved him and how strong he had been through all these problems. I told him that things would get better soon with Tilly, or she would have to leave. I did want to help our little girl, but I couldn't sacrifice my own child in the process. Charlie knew that his dad was the one insisting that Tilly stay, and he wondered aloud what would happen if things didn't change soon. Neither of us had an answer to that......

About the same time that I began doing the play therapy with Tilly, I began talking to several other foster and adoptive parents who were having some of the same problems with their children from the state that I was having with Tilly. One woman had a little boy who showed the same kind of intense anger and defiance that I was seeing in Tilly. This mom said she thought her son had Reactive Attachment Disorder. She had heard a radio program about this condition and said it completely explained her son's inability to bond with her and also his extreme behavior. I had never heard this term before, but had heard about babies having trouble in life if they never formed a good attachment to their mothers.

As I thought about it, an attachment disorder actually seemed like it might fit for our little girl, too. Tilly had been an only child and was born when her mother was very young, so her mom probably didn't have a lot of experience with babies. Tilly's parents were involved with drugs, domestic violence, and arrests the whole time she was with them, so it seemed likely that she didn't have a very normal upbringing. In this type of environment, it would have been hard for her to form a good attachment to either parent.

Tilly had been taken from her parents by the state at age two and had lived with a series of foster families, but only for two weeks or so at a time. (From the information that we received from the state, long after Tilly had been placed with us, it had been noted that these first foster placements had all failed due to Tilly's violent behavior.) She had finally been placed with her aunt and uncle where she had lived for the past two years. It was very obvious that Tilly had not formed any attachment to her aunt, uncle or cousin, so it didn't look like there had been anyone in her short life that she had been able to become close with.

Attachment disorder would certainly explain why Tilly had not felt any sadness when she left her relatives. This warning sign, something that even I had noticed, should have been identified by our case worker, or the case worker I spoke to at the foster care picnic, and should have been immediately addressed. It seemed like our county just wasn't aware of the serious problems and family disruptions that would occur when children suffering from this issue were placed with a new family.

The adoptive mom who told me about attachment disorder offered to lend me an audio tape of the radio program she had heard. The program was a talk by someone in the field who was successful in working with these kinds of kids. This helpful mom told me that the tape not only explained her son's behavior, it also had good suggestions for helping him. I couldn't wait to hear the tape myself!

Chapter 7 - Reactive Attachment Disorder

The afternoon I listened to the tape, I became hopeful that there really was a solution for Tilly. The man on the recording described how children who had never formed a loving attachment to anyone experienced an intense interior rage. These kids had often grown up without having someone to consistently change them when they needed a new diaper, cuddle them when they were lonely, or feed them when they were hungry. They would cry out for help, but often no one would come.

These babies would grow into young children who knew they could not count on the adults in their lives. They would urinate inappropriately, even after they were fully potty trained, as a way to express their anger with the world. They seemed to enjoy creating chaos, especially when they felt that people were trying to become close to them. These kids didn't feel safe allowing the closeness that they actually craved, because they knew they would eventually be abandoned. Chaos and destruction gave these kids some power over their surroundings. These were things that they could control which seemed to give them some sense of pleasure.

Wow!!!! This all made sense. From Tilly's point of view, she was trying to prevent us from becoming too close to her, because it would hurt that much more when we eventually rejected her. The speaker's suggestion that these kids "urinated out their anger" was also astonishing. Tilly did frequently urinate, seemingly intentionally, when she wasn't happy about something. She had so many accidents when she was changing her clothes that I finally made a rule that she had to change clothes in the bathroom. I didn't know why she was having these accidents, but at least the bathroom was easier to clean up than the carpet in her room. I had also noticed that she sometimes peed all over the toilet seat, but had thought she just wasn't paying attention. This idea of expressing anger by peeing on things certainly gave me a different perspective.

The radio program had not just described the symptoms of this disorder, it also talked about a way to cure it. The child needed to be held and rocked while the adult looked lovingly into their eyes. The idea was to recreate the early closeness that most children get as babies. I was so excited to finally have something to try! Maybe we could help Tilly overcome her behavior issues and finally adopt the delightful little girl we had gotten to know the first few weeks she had been with us. Maybe there was hope after all..........

As soon as the taped program came to an end, it was time for me to go pick up the kids from their schools. I picked up Charlie first and excitedly told him that I thought I finally knew why Tilly was acting the way she was. I told him that there were things that I could do that might really help Tilly become a happier girl. Charlie surprised me with his response. He said he was glad there was a way to help her. He then added, "I sure hope we can fix her."

Although he was certainly suffering and his home life had become very difficult, Charlie was hoping that there was a way to help his little sister. It seemed so odd to me at the time, and still does now, that little Charlie, who felt the brunt of the anger and abuse from Tilly, was so ready to help her, so hopeful that she could feel better. If I had been in his place, I would have been begging my parents to send her away and give me back my normal life.

Later that evening up in the barn, after I had finished feeding the animals, I called Tilly over to me. I remember sitting on the cold cement stairs and looking up into the dark sky at all the twinkling stars. As I held Tilly on my lap, I prayed that the new information I had just learned was going to help. "I just want to look into your eyes Tilly," I said quietly, as I held her in my arms and softly rocked her back and forth. "You have such beautiful brown eyes, just like mine." Tilly looked back into my eyes for only a second, and then looked away.

"I can't look, Mommy," she said.

The man from the radio program had said that most babies are held and rocked by their caretakers when they are young and establish a loving eye-to-eye contact with that person, usually their mom. He said there is something deep and life-changing about this loving, soft, eye contact that helps establish the human connection that we all need to have good, loving social relationships. Babies that don't ever get this connection somehow can't seem to form close relationships and this can persist for their whole life.

The man on the recording said to check to see if the child can maintain this kind of soft eye contact. Children with attachment disorder won't be able to do this. They can't maintain that kind of closeness and connectedness with anyone. He said the solution to this problem, and the way to help children with this disorder, is to hold them on your lap (whatever their age) rock (in a rocking chair) and help them feel safe enough that they can learn to trust you. He said eventually all kids can make this loving eye-to-eye connection, and then their lives can start to change.

Tilly had just given me the answer to my question. She did seem to have this disorder, but thankfully, now I knew about a cure. I planned to order the book the man on the radio program spoke about...... and Tilly and I were going to start rocking!

Over the next few months, I would have my rocking time with Tilly every day, usually right after lunch and before her nap. We would sit in my big recliner that rocked and I would sing her a made-up song. "Mommy loves Tilly, Tilly is Mommy's baby," I would sing as we rocked. I would look into her eyes and didn't mind that she couldn't return my gaze very often. After she went up to take her nap, I would play the same tune I had been singing, on the piano, so she could hear it as she dropped off to sleep.

At first Tilly was a little resistant about our rocking time and would struggle to leave very quickly. I told her we only needed to rock for a few minutes and would let go as soon as she wanted to get up. As she climbed down, however long she had stayed in my lap, I would always say that she did great and that I had sure enjoyed sitting with her. Although I could see that the special play time and rocking were starting to have an effect on Tilly, we continued to have lots of struggles.

Chapter 8 - Logical Consequences

As soon as I received the book that I had ordered, *When Love Is Not Enough: A guide to Parenting Children with Reactive Attachment Disorder*, by Nancy L. Thomas, I read it and began using some of the suggestions. Tilly already had accepted that I wouldn't give in to tantrums and screaming, but now I had some good ways to help her make better choices. The book described how to use logical consequences to help a child understand how their choices were affecting what they were able to do; I immediately began trying this out with Tilly.

One Sunday morning, when Tilly refused to put on her shoes to go to Sunday School (which was somewhere she really liked to go) I told her that she'd have to stay home if she didn't put her shoes on right away. Bill and Charlie were ready to go and, when she didn't make an effort to put her shoes on, I said "Good bye" to them and they drove off without us. Tilly then had an explosion about not getting to go. I calmly explained that next time she could decide to put on her shoes and she would get to go. My angry little girl glared at me, but did stop screaming and did seem to understand.

Another day Tilly was having a hard time with everything, it seemed. She had just wet her second pair of blue jeans, so I left her in the bathroom and went up to her room to get more pants. There was only one pair left in the drawer, and they were definitely not her favorite ones. As I handed them to her back in the bathroom, she began to yell. It was the hated green jeans! These were hand-me-downs from Charlie and were her least favorite pants in the world. She had newer jeans to wear to school and other blue jeans for at home; these she mainly wore when we were working in the garden. Tilly screamed that she didn't want to wear the green jeans. I tried to stay calm as I explained that they were the only ones left and she would need to wear them today. It was hard to be sympathetic while holding two sodden, dripping pairs in my other hand that had been clean only moments before.

  Tilly finally got dressed and put on her coat and shoes. We went outside and she played on the swings as I worked in the yard. Everything was calm for almost an hour, then she suddenly cried out that she had wet her pants and needed to go in and change. I was not the least bit happy with this news. I guessed that Tilly thought she had found a way to not have to wear the green pants after all. I stopped for a minute and thought. I didn't want her controlling the situation this way. I certainly didn't want to reward her for having another "accident" by finding something else for her to wear. What would be a logical consequence..............................

  An idea finally came to me as I looked at the red-faced little girl who was standing there with a triumphant look on her face. I had Tilly go to the bathroom and take off the wet pants and then told her she'd need to take a shower and get cleaned up. "What am I going to wear?" she asked.

"I'll tell you when you're all done," I said.

I then left a clean pair of underwear, socks and t-shirt out for Tilly. When she was out of the shower and had gotten as dressed as she could, I told her she'd have to go up and stay in her bed until I could wash and dry the green pants. Over her angry howls, I explained that she had already been told that she was going to wear the green pants that day and would now have to wait until they were clean again. Tilly finally decided that there was no point in arguing and went up and read books in bed. I went up an hour and a half later with her green jeans and laid them on the bed. Tilly didn't say a word but got dressed and came down stairs. As I recall there were very few "accidents" afterwards. Using logical consequences was working!

One other time the logical consequences idea worked especially well was in our conflict over lunches at preschool. The preschool Tilly attended provided lunch for the children, but it was not very nutritious. They usually served white bread with spaghetti on top, or something similar that was very starchy. The school didn't have vegetables or fruit available most of the time either. I wanted Tilly to have a better balanced meal, so I would pack her a lunch. Once a week, usually on Friday, she could eat their lunch, but the rest of the time she would take a sack lunch from home.

Tilly preferred what the school served and would sometimes try to leave her lunch sack in the car I learned to always check the car before driving away from her school, so eventually this trick stopped working. One day Tilly left her lunch in the house, but I noticed it as I was locking the door and went back inside to get the sack. When we got to school, though, there was no lunch sack to be found in the car. I looked everywhere while Tilly struggled to get out of her car seat so she could run inside to preschool. I finally realized that she must have dropped the lunch sack out of the car before we left the house. I wasn't sure how this had happened, but it seemed to be the only explanation.

I explained to Tilly that this wasn't a day that she could have school lunch, so we'd have to drive back home to get her lunch. I also told her that this was wasting Mommy's time, so she would have extra chores when she got home to make up for the time I was spending going back for her lunch. I didn't let Tilly go in to school but had her accompany me home. We drove home, picked up the lunch from the carport and then returned to school. Tilly was mad that she had missed the first part of her class and angrily grabbed her sack and stomped into school with me.

When we got home that afternoon, I gave her a large basket of laundry to fold, and she worked on it without complaining. When she was done, I gave her a big hug and thanked her for her help. "Next time, lets make sure your lunch gets to school with you," I said. Tilly looked up at me and nodded. It was amazing how it made sense, even to a 4 year old, that leaving that lunch home hadn't been worth it.

Another idea I liked from the book was not blaming the child when they weren't listening to you. Instead of becoming angry and repeating things over and over to the non-listening child, the book suggested that the child must not be able to listen because they needed to have more oxygen getting to their brain. I would explain to Tilly that she needed to do some jumping jacks so her brain got enough oxygen that she would be able to listen to Mommy. After she had exercised for a few minutes, I would ask if she had enough oxygen to be able to listen. I loved this idea of not getting angry, not punishing the child, but merely helping the child do something so that they would be able to listen. Tilly thought doing jumping jacks was kind of silly, but we both found that it usually did work.

Something else we found useful from *When Love is Not Enough*, was a way to help Tilly when she became frustrated. In the past Tilly would throw toys or smash things when her internal emotions go out of control, but now we had a much better solution. I would have her run laps around the back yard and would watch from the kitchen window and count how many times she circled the yard. Sometimes Tilly would even suggest running herself, when she wasn't feeling OK. She would ask me to go to the window and count for her, which I was happy to do. After running two or three times around the big yard, she would come in, slightly out of breath, feeling much calmer and happier. Tilly had found a way to calm herself down that was not destructive and was actually good for her health. Tilly was finding ways to help herself feel better!

One very interesting thing I learned over time about our little girl, was how well she was able to behave if told to stay within a specific boundary. She had great difficulty with so many other things, but when I told her to stay somewhere, she would actually stay there. I first found this out when I would ask Tilly to wait on the stairs in the barn or in the sunroom for a few minutes while I finished something. She would also stay in her little chair in the stall at the barn even when she was angry and wanted to go back to the house. However, when she was to stay in the larger area of the stall, even though there were toys and dolls to play with, she had proceeded to smash things. It seemed like it was somehow reassuring to her to have one small place to be where she knew she would be OK.

Using a boundary had also worked well at Christmas when I finally put tape on the living room carpet that she wasn't to cross to prevent her from pulling over the tree. This had worked so well that later I marked off an area in the living room, again with tape, for her to play where there was no furniture for her to damage. She actually seemed very content when I had her go to her little area with a toy or her coloring book to play by herself for awhile. I could get things done in the kitchen, or pay bills at the dining room table and Tilly could easily see me, and have a safe spot to be. I have no idea if other children who have issues similar to Tilly's would react well to having a small, safe place to play, but it certainly worked well for us.

Chapter 9 - Attachment

The weeks went by and we continued with our daily rocking sessions. Although, at first, Tilly hadn't been able to rock with me very long, now she would stay in my lap longer and longer. Finally, after several months, she was not only able to look back into my eyes as I looked into hers, she was able to return my soft gaze. Instead of seeing the dark, hateful glare that I used to see when she was being resistant, I saw a new openness. When I looked in her eyes now, I saw a beautiful, little girl who hadn't been loved enough as a baby and who had been struggling, so hard, to try to get along in this scary, unpredictable world. In Tilly's soft, dark brown eyes, I now saw love and acceptance. It was absolutely amazing!

As Tilly made this huge leap of faith in accepting someone into her life, I began to see wonderful changes in her. I often took Tilly grocery shopping with me and had tried, unsuccessfully, early on to have her help me carry the lighter-weight bags in from the car when we got home. Tilly had found it great fun to grab a bag and then drop it "accidentally" into a mud puddle on the way to the house. I quickly learned that it was safer to just carry everything myself. One day, though, Tilly acted like she really did want to help me. We had just returned from the store with lots of groceries, and she eagerly offered to help. I kind of held my breath, but went ahead and handed Tilly a bag to carry. She carried one bag after another across the driveway, up the stairs, and into the kitchen without any mishaps and seemed glad that she had made me happy. "What a wonderful helper you are!" I exclaimed as I gave her a big hug. Tilly looked up at me and smiled.

What was going on here? How could an angry child change just by rocking her and looking into her eyes? This wouldn't last, would it? I had been hoping and praying that Tilly would get better, but I hadn't really dared believe that it could really happen.

Tilly didn't change overnight, but the changes did start, rather suddenly, and a much happier, calmer child appeared. One difference I noticed right away was Tilly's new concern for me. In the past Tilly had enjoyed any kind of problem that I had. If I spilled something in the kitchen, she would laugh at the resulting mess. It had seemed to delight her that I now had more work to do. These days, though, if I dropped something or there was a big noise in the kitchen, Tilly would come running in to see if I was OK. One day I dropped a big bag of frozen blueberries and they scattered like marbles all over the kitchen floor. My little girl came running in saying, "Let me help you, Mommy." She crawled around on the floor with me hunting for those berries, reaching her small arm under the refrigerator and feeling to see if any had rolled there.

As much as I enjoyed this much happier, kinder girl, I did notice that her behavior hadn't changed much towards Charlie. The afternoon of Charlie's birthday party, Tilly and I were in the kitchen getting his cake ready. Tilly decided she wanted to make a special birthday card for her brother and spent a long time carefully coloring a picture to paste on the front of the card. "Charlie is really nice to me," Tilly said as she drew her picture. I agreed with her and asked if it was hard for her to be nice to Charlie. She nodded and kept working on the card.

I had noticed that Tilly would do nice things for Charlie and talk about him in a positive way, as long as he wasn't home. Once he came home, though, her attitude would completely change. She just didn't seem to be able to stop glaring at him or acting very rudely towards him when we were all together. This just didn't make sense to me. Tilly's behavior towards me was now so much better. Why hadn't it gotten better towards Charlie too?

One afternoon as Tilly and I were driving in the car to go pick up Charlie after school, Tilly said something that gave me my answer. Tilly said, "Mommy, if you just had me things would be so much easier for you. You could take me to school and then ride your horses and have lunch and then come to get me. Things would be so much nicer......."

"But Tilly," I said. "That just can't happen."

"I know," Tilly said sadly, "But I need it to be that way."

Thinking about what Tilly had just said made me finally understand. Tilly had never had a real mom before, and now that she had someone who was able love her, she needed me all to herself. She wasn't able to be nice to Charlie because she didn't want to have to share her mother.

Despite Tilly's reluctance to share me with Charlie, her attachment to me definitively made things much better at our house. Tilly, in general, seemed much more relaxed these days. She was becoming a happier little person who wanted to spend lots of time with Mommy. She began helping me more in the kitchen, and surprisingly, was now better up at the barn too. She had also stopped lying to me about things (but still did tell lies to Bill) and genuinely seemed to want to please me. I still had to watch her around our dogs and the rabbit, but her aggression towards the pets seemed to be fading.

I had also begun to notice that Tilly was doing much better at taking care of her toys. She was now able to pick up her toys in the living room when I asked, and as a result, I tried putting a few toys in her room as well. She just didn't seem to have that same anger, most of the time, that drove her to smash and break things. I was so happy to see these changes, but there was still something that didn't seem right.

Each time Tilly would be doing really well for a week or more and I began thinking that we had finally gotten things smoothed out for her, she would then have several days of chaotic behavior. On these days it seemed like she was reverting back to her previous, angry self. Of course, all kids have good and bad days, and little Tilly had been going through all kinds of transitions and changes. She was, after all, now only 5 years old, but still, her behavior changes just weren't making sense.

I had continued keeping up with my journal every day, and it became apparent when I looked back that the stretches of good days were always followed by several really defiant days. If I hadn't been taking notes, I'm not sure that I would have seen it, but there was definitely a pattern in her cycles of behavior. I checked to make sure it wasn't just the less structured weekends that were creating the more difficult days, but that didn't seem to be the case.

I knew from Tilly's aunt and uncle that there was a family history of alcohol and drug dependence, and also a history of mental illness. There seemed to have been quite a few relatives with depression, and also several with bi-polar disorder. I didn't know much about bi-polar, but knew it did involve cycles of up and down moods. Now that Tilly was a happier, calmer little girl, perhaps it was more noticeable that she was having these cycles in her behavior and mood. Maybe we could get some medication to help with the agitation that she seemed to be experiencing during her days of anger and defiance. Perhaps this would be the final piece of the puzzle. If we could just get a little help for this issue, we could finally adopt Tilly and really become a family.

Just as I was puzzling over this new problem with Tilly, we received an inch- thick manilla envelope from Tilly's case worker. The envelope included pages and pages of details about Tilly's parents along with their arrest records and also some additional background information about our daughter. It became clear as I read through the papers that this was information that we should have received when we were selected as one of the final three possible families for Tilly. All the families were supposed to receive a copy of her complete file so that they would know more about the child that might soon become part of their family. At the very least, this information should have been sent when we were chosen to be her new family. Somehow, though, it hadn't reached us until now.

    The thing that I found the most disturbing, in that whole stack of papers, was a page describing the type of family that would best suit Tilly. It clearly stated that she should not go to a family with other children in the home due to her high need for attention and aggressive tendencies. It made me angry to read that sentence. Someone had known that placing her in a home with another child might be dangerous, and yet we had been selected to adopt her! All of the struggles and anguish might have been avoided for our family if that instruction had been heeded. I decided, after I calmed down, to not let this new knowledge stand in the way of helping our little girl. Instead, I began trying to figure out how to find someone who could tell us about bi-polar disorder.

Chapter 10 - The Children's Hospital Evaluation

It had been almost 9 months since Tilly came to live with us when I received a phone call from our case worker telling me that Tilly was now scheduled for her evaluation at the Children's Hospital. They would see us next week! I was so excited that we'd finally have some professionals to talk to about our little girl! I had only recently noticed Tilly's odd mood cycles, and now I could get a mental health specialist to tell us what to do.

When I called the hospital to confirm our appointment, I was told that we were going to spend a whole day at the Children's Hospital with a team of doctors and psychologists. They would ask me background information about Tilly and then do a full medical and psychological examination. These were the people who would know what to do to help our little girl. I quickly called Bill at his office to tell him the good news.

As I was preparing for this long-awaited visit to the hospital, I went back through my notes about Tilly, as well as the new information that we had just received, and began typing up a summary. Bill wouldn't be able to go with us for the evaluation, so I wanted him to read through what I had written and give me his input too. My husband and I hadn't always agreed on the best ways to help Tilly or even if we should keep her, so I wanted him to be involved as much as possible in this big evaluation.

As Bill read through my several pages of information, he seemed, for the first time, to be able to see the difficulties I had been dealing with for over eight months. Seeing things presented in a non-emotional, factual way made an impact on him, and suddenly we seemed to be on the same page about our girl. I had listed all the background information we had on Tilly's parents and relatives, her behavior when she first arrived, and the progression we had seen of anger and destructiveness. I also listed the recent improvements Tilly had made and her new ability to show care and concern for me.

What stood out the most to both of us were her odd cycles of up and down moods and her continued dislike of our son. If we could get help in these two areas, we both felt that we could actually makes thing work. It was such a huge relief to feel like Bill and I were finally a team again. For such a long time I had felt mostly alone in my struggles to help Tilly.

As the date of the evaluation drew closer, I spent some time talking to Charlie about what would happen that day. I was expecting to spend the whole day at the hospital, so I wouldn't be picking him up at school like I always did. Instead, a friend would drive him home from school and he'd stay with his grandmother until we got home. Charlie and I talked about the doctors at the hospital who evaluated thousands of kids each year. They would probably know just what we could do to help Tilly become a happy part of the family. Charlie was worn out from his constant battles with Tilly but was very hopeful that soon things would be much better.

It was on a cool, clear Thursday morning that Tilly and I set out for the city. We had a long drive ahead of us, and I was a bit worried about finding our way to the correct location at the hospital. I had been sent a rather complicated-looking map that showed where we were supposed to go once we reached the huge hospital. There were lots of buildings, walkways, and parking lots set in a snarl of one-way city streets. For a country girl like me, this was rather intimidating. Luckily, we found the correct parking lot without too much trouble and arrived right on time for Tilly's appointment.

Tilly was excited about our trip to the city and the promised lunch at a restaurant. I had told her she would be meeting lots of nice doctors and that she should do just what they told her and answer all of their questions. As we walked up to the counter to check in, Tilly squealed with excitement. There were toys all around the waiting area, including an oversize, beautiful wooden rocking horse. Tilly climbed right up on the horse and happily rocked while I gave the receptionist her name and signed several papers.

A nurse called us back right away to a cheerful examination room and explained what would be happening the rest of the day. She said I would be meeting with one psychologist while she took Tilly to another room to do some testing and to talk to a second psychologist. Then we would both meet with the medical doctor who would do a full physical and determine if there were any medical concerns with Tilly. We would have an hour to get lunch at one of the cafeterias and then would come back for hearing and vision tests. At the end of the afternoon, I would meet with the whole team to hear their conclusions. I was now as excited as Tilly was. I would know something by the end of the day!

    I gave my typed notes to the psychologist when he came in and then spent over an hour going through Tilly's history while she was living with us, and as much as I knew of her earlier life. The psychologist seemed very thorough and had lots of questions for me. Then he had me fill out several questionnaires about our child's behavior, personality, and relationship skills. After about two hours, I met up with Tilly again for the medical evaluation. Tilly was still cheerful and had thought the testing she had done with puzzles and shapes was fun. She wasn't happy about opening her mouth for the doctor or removing her clothes, but the doctor was a very pleasant woman who tried to make everything fun.

    The exam finished up with the doctor having Tilly get dressed and then inviting us to go with her to a big room that was set up like a gym. There were large baskets sitting around the room filled with various types of balls and gymnastic-type mats spread out on the floor. One wall was completely covered with mirrors and I also noticed some very low balance beams. The doctor had Tilly throw and catch a ball, walk on her tip toes, and balance on first one foot and then the other. The doctor eventually pronounced

Tilly healthy and fit and said she had pretty good coordination for her age. The doctor then said we were free for the next hour and suggested that we go find some lunch.

Tilly and I set off to explore the many buildings of the hospital which were connected by long, elevated walkways. We found a nice, bright lunchroom that wasn't too crowded and Tilly picked out a huge hamburger, chips and ice cream from the cafeteria line. I wasn't sure she'd be able to eat that much, but she did. "I sure was hungry", she told me. She also said that she was so glad it was just us that had come today. I told her that I was glad too.

We both really enjoyed our day together. The little girl that Tilly was becoming was such a change from the defiant, difficult girl she'd been only a short time ago. The day at the hospital was almost like her coming out party! Lots of attention by so many people, a fun time at lunch, and she had Mommy all to herself for the entire day.

We eventually headed back to the children's area of the hospital to finish our appointments. Tilly's vision and hearing checked out in the normal range and soon a young woman came to take Tilly so that I could talk to the evaluation team by myself. As they went out the door, I could hear Tilly requesting that they go to the lobby to ride the giant rocking horse.

Soon the professionals with their white coats trooped into the room where I was waiting. I was so anxious to hear what they had decided! What could we do to help Tilly with her few remaining problems? They were all smiling at me, but I sensed that there was something else, something that I might not want to hear. The psychologist whom I had first talked to began. He said that they thought I'd done a great job with Tilly so far and thought she'd continue to improve with consistent parenting. They thought that her attachment issues had been mostly resolved, but did think that she probably had bi-polar disorder.

However, he went on to say, the team couldn't recommend any medication at this point to help with her fluctuating moods. The psychologist said they would need several months of documentation about her mood cycles and behavior changes on their special forms before they could suggest a helpful drug. He explained that they needed this type of specific documentation for a diagnosis and also to determine how well any medications they prescribed in the future were working.

My happy, hopeful mood evaporated. I suddenly began to feel very sad and very tired. It would be very hard for me, and especially for Charlie, to manage for three more months without any help for Tilly during her chaotic, difficult days. We needed something to help us now! I asked if there was anything at all that they could suggest that we could try right away. The medical doctor told me that a nutritious diet was always helpful, but thought that Tilly was already eating very healthy food, so there really wasn't anything to change.

As I sat there considering what I'd just heard, I thought that if we could stop Tilly's anger towards Charlie, maybe we could handle waiting for help with her mood cycles. The female psychologist, who had spent time with Tilly that day, then began to speak. She said that she would be addressing my second concern: Improving the relationship between Tilly and Charlie. As the blond-haired woman rose from her chair, she gave me a rather forced smile. She then said, "In my professional opinion, I don't think Tilly will ever accept having Charlie as a sibling." The psychologist explained that because of Tilly's past history of very unstable relationships, and also her individual personality, she would do best as an only child.

I didn't know what to say. I just stared at the psychologist. What had this professional, whom we had waited so many months to see, just told me? How could she be saying this! Why wasn't she telling us what we should do to fix things between the kids? Finally, I was able to talk. "What are we supposed to do?" I asked. "She can't be an only child in our family."

The psychologist said she was just telling me what would be best for Tilly. "Obviously," she went on to say, "your family will have to make your own decisions about what to do." The psychologist said that from an attachment standpoint, it would be best for Tilly to stay with us, but that it wasn't healthy for her to live in a household with another child at this time. She explained that having another child in the house brought out very negative emotions in Tilly. It would be best for Tilly's mental health to live in a household where she didn't need to compete for attention from her parents.

I felt numb as I thanked the team for their help and walked out to the waiting room to find Tilly. There she was, waiting for me on the big horse, with a huge smile on her face. She had enjoyed her day in the city with Mommy. This child, who had been through so much, had no idea that the friendly doctors and psychologists had given us a verdict that would mean the end of our family of four.

Tilly fell asleep on the way home and I appreciated the quietness. I could only hear the hum of the engine and the sound of the tires on the road. I needed time to process everything that had happened at the hospital. My mind was spinning with so many thoughts. How would we ever tell Tilly that she would have to leave us? How would Bill react to this news? I felt that all my efforts to help our little girl be happy had been for nothing. What would she think as she grew up? Would she ever understand what an important part of my life she had been? What would happen now?

As I drove along the highway, I glanced back at Tilly asleep in her car seat. She was exhausted after her long, eventful day. She looked so relaxed and peaceful leaning against her headrest, with her tousled hair hanging across her face. She also looked so very young, so very small.

When we arrived at home that evening, I carried Tilly up to her room and laid her gently on her bed. Her eyes fluttered open a few times as I tucked her in, but then she fell back to sleep. I walked up the hill to the barn to take care of the animals and met

Charlie halfway up the driveway. He had been playing ball with his grandmother and ran over when he saw me. "What happened?" he asked.

I continued walking up the hill with Charlie hopping along at my side. He had a hopeful look on his face. He was expecting me to tell him that the doctors at the hospital knew just what to do. I took a breath and told him that it would be several months before we could get any medicine to help Tilly. Then I told him that the doctors didn't think that she would be able to stay with us.

Charlie's happy expression suddenly changed. He now looked very serious. "I was hoping that they could help her," he said softly. I hugged my kind son and told him that I had been hoping the same thing. Charlie helped me feed the horses and then we walked back down to the house. Charlie was very quiet. I could tell just what he was thinking–he was sad that his little sister wouldn't be able to stay,

When we got to the house I asked Charlie not to talk about any of this with Tilly. "I'll need to talk to your dad and to her case worker before we tell her anything," I said. "I'm not sure what is going to happen now......."

Later in the evening, Bill got home from work and asked how it had gone at the hospital. I explained what had happened, and what their final opinion had been. Bill couldn't believe it.. The doctors had come to the same conclusion as the report we had recently read from Tilly's case file: Tilly would need to live with a family where she could be an only child. "We should have been told this a long time ago!" Bill shouted. "They should not have chosen us as her family!" Bill was as angry and frustrated about the situation as I was. We had struggled so hard for the past nine months to help our little girl become part of our family, and now it seemed like it had all been for nothing. She needed a different family.........

As I sat in the sunroom late that evening looking up into the dark, night sky, our collie, who always knew if anyone was feeling sad, came over and lay down next to me. Her warm, furry body pressed up against me as she rested her long face on my leg. She looked up at me with her friendly, brown eyes. As I stroked her soft head, I thought back about everything that had happened. I remembered that first day when Tilly had sat on my lap, and just like Kelly was doing now, she had leaned up against me and relaxed. I loved my little girl and truly wanted her to be happy, but it would be so hard to let her go.

As I sat there petting the dog and looking at the stars, I realized that the psychologist today had been right, Tilly really would need a new family. It was especially sad, I thought, that just as Tilly was beginning to bloom and become a more secure, happy little girl, she would need to leave us. It would be very hard for all of us to break up the family we had struggled to create, but this time, when Tilly embarked on her new journey, she would leave behind people that she loved and who loved her. I hoped that the progress we had made would help her have a much easier experience in her next home. She was not the same child we had met nine months ago. She was now a little girl who was ready to be part of a family.

Chapter 11 - Saying Good Bye

I called our case worker the next day. She was very surprised to hear what the Children's Hospital had told us and seemed equally surprised that their decision would mean that Tilly would need to find another home. She asked that Bill and I come to her office the next day to discuss the situation.

When we arrived for our appointment the next day, we found that the psychologist who had taught me how to do the parent-child play therapy was there as well. She and the case worker asked if some counseling might help put the adoption back on track. Why on earth would they be offering counseling now, I wondered? Why hadn't they tried to help us more before, when we were desperate for some help? Bill told them that this wasn't a case of trying to put out a little barn fire. He looked straight at the two women and shouted, "The barn has already burned down!"

We explained that Tilly probably did have some type of mood disorder that could eventually be treated, but that the psychologists didn't think she would ever be OK living in a household with another child. "We care about both Tilly and Charlie too much to continue something that is bad for both of them," I said. "Tilly is ready for a forever family now. She certainly wasn't when she came to us, but she is now. Aren't there any couples that would like to have a smart, wonderful little girl?" We told our case worker that we would be happy to have Tilly with us until they could find just the right family for her. We really wanted her to find a perfect home.

Several days later the case worker called to say that there was an opening at a foster home where difficult children were often sent. I protested this choice. "Tilly doesn't need that kind of setting," I said. "She just needs a home without other children." The case worker, who had never really listened to my idea that Tilly was suffering from Reactive Attachment Disorder before, now seemed to think that Tilly should be sent to tough foster parents who could work on her behavior. "Tilly is past that now," I told the case worker. "She is ready for a family."

Although I don't think the case worker was very happy about the placement she was eventually able to arrange for Tilly, I thought it sounded perfect. Tilly was to go to a married couple who had one of their parents living with them as well. Tilly would have parents and a grandparent, and be the only child in the home.

The case worker explained that the couple had just finished their foster parenting classes and had never had a foster child before. She added that they were hoping to find a child that they could adopt. Wow! I thought this sounded great! Tilly would be the only child with three adults to give her attention and support. I had a good feeling about her new home.

Bill and I received pictures of Tilly's new parents and were told that we could call and tell them all about Tilly and answer their questions. I called that day and tried to give them as much advice as I could about the things that had worked best in taking care of our special girl. I also promised to give them the book that had helped me so much. I mostly spoke to the wife, and she sounded as anxious and excited as I had been before Tilly came to live with us. I told her that we would bring Tilly's many toys and all her belongings when the transition took place, but that Tilly would probably do much better if they put most of her things away for awhile, like we did, so that she wouldn't be overwhelmed.

Finally the day arrived to tell Tilly the news. The case worker arrived in the morning and our whole family gathered in the living room. Tilly hadn't seen the case worker for over 6 months and wondered why she was at our house. The case worker explained that she was there to talk to us. She told Tilly that she had some important things to say. The woman looked to make sure that Tilly was listening and then turned to her and said that it wasn't going to work out for her to stay with us. She told Tilly that she was going to have a different forever home. Tilly immediately whirled around and ran to me.

"It's because I can't be nice to Charlie, isn't it?" she asked. I put my arms around her and held her close.

"It's not your fault," I said. "It will just be better for you if you don't have any brothers or sisters for awhile."

"Where will I go?" she asked while sinking down onto the floor.

I picked her up and put her on my lap. "The case worker found nice people who really want to have a little girl," I said. I showed her the picture of a smiling middle-aged couple. "They don't have any children and are very sad about it. I know they will be very happy to have you come to live with them."

I turned Tilly around so I could look into her eyes. "You are a wonderful little girl and need to be in a home where you don't feel angry about things." I hugged her to me and said quietly, "We love you so much. We want you to be in a place where you can be happy."

We all drove down later that day to meet her new foster parents. Tilly and Charlie explored the back yard and the house while we talked to the new parents. Both parents seemed very excited to meet Tilly. They asked if it would be OK for her to move to their house the next day. Things were happening so fast now. It was hard to believe that in one more day Tilly would really be gone!

I gave Tilly's new parents my copy of *When Love is not Enough* and also the notes that I had typed up for the Children's Hospital. I wanted them to have the best chance of success and wanted to share the things that we had ended up learning the hard way. We all felt it would be helpful for Tilly to stick to the rules she was used to and to try to maintain her same daily schedule, as much as possible, after she moved. Her new parents were extremely cooperative and seemed happy to hear all we had to say.

After we got back home, Tilly and I went up to her room to start packing. We had lots to do before she left the next day. It was a very sad afternoon as we sorted through her drawers and closet and made piles of clothing to pack that still fit, and other piles of things that were now too small.

After we had everything sorted, Tilly was surprised to see me walk into her room with two very large, colorful suitcases. This time Tilly would not be moving with her things thrown in garbage bags! Charlie's grandmother had given us two beautiful suitcases that were covered with pink and red flowers. Tilly was amazed that these were her suitcases to take with her and to keep. I told her that things really would be different this time.

As dinner time approached, I told Tilly that she could pick anything that she wanted to have for dinner and could pick out a movie to watch later too. Charlie had gone to spend the night with his grandmother, so Tilly got to spend her last evening just with us. We all tried to enjoy our dinner of hot dogs and macaroni and cheese, but there was a heavy feeling all around us. We watched a Disney movie later and had big bowls of ice cream with chocolate syrup. After dinner we gave Tilly a new photo album that I had put together with pictures of all of us, our farm, and the animals. I had wanted her to be able to see us whenever she wanted to and remember her time with our family.

Just before bedtime, Tilly and I went down to rock in my big recliner one last time. We rocked for a long time, but I found I couldn't sing. My throat felt thick and tears kept coming to my eyes. Rocking in this old chair had brought about wonderful changes for Tilly. She had finally learned to trust someone, to care about someone else, and to allow herself to be loved. I prayed that she would let her new parents love her too.

Epilogue

Tilly called us often after she moved to her new home, but her parents eventually thought it was best for the calls to stop. Mom explained that Tilly still missed us and wanted to return to our home. She said that Tilly would cry after her calls and would remain upset for the rest of the day. Despite what our case worker had thought, Tilly had become attached to us and was very sad about having to leave. It was hard for me to think about her sadness, but I did feel encouraged to know that she now had the ability to form attachments. Hopefully, very soon, Tilly would bond with her new family and be able to enjoy a happy, stable childhood.

Although we weren't able to stay in touch with the little five year-old who had been such a part of our lives, we did hear from her new case worker occasionally. About a year after Tilly joined her new family, we heard that they were in the process of adopting her.

As I think back now about those months that Tilly was with us, I mostly remember how wonderful it was to see her begin to change. I remember the first time she was able to return my loving gaze while we rocked, and her new ability to be kind. To have a child who wanted to create chaos and hurt things become a loving little girl who wanted to spend time with Mommy and give me lots of hugs, was so amazing..... It was a life changing experience, not only for Tilly, but also for me.

Even though Tilly can no longer be a part of my life, I still have the little stuffed dog that she gave me for Christmas that year. It sits on a shelf in my room and I see it every night as I get ready for bed. The cute little dog in the Santa hat hasn't changed over the years, but the little girl who gave it to me certainly did. She became a child who was able to be loved and she finally found her forever home.

References

Suess, Dr. (1963). *Hop on Pop*. New York: Random House.

Thomas, Nancy L. (2005). *When Love Is Not Enough: A Guide to Parenting Children with Reactive Attachment Disorder*. Glenwood Springs, CO: Families by Design Inc.

Printed in Great Britain
by Amazon.co.uk, Ltd.,
Marston Gate.